Carmel, 12/2000

to A...

With dedication,

Amelia

The Garden
of My Childhood

The Garden
of My Childhood

by

Aurelia

RIVERCROSS PUBLISHING, INC.
Orlando

ISBN: 1-58141-019-0

Library of Congress Catalog Card Number: 00-35283

First Printing

Library of Congress Cataloging-in-Publication Data

Aurelia.
   The garden of my childhood / by Aurelia
      p. cm.
   ISBN 1-58141-019-0
      I.   Title

PS509.D6 A96 2000
811'.6—dc21

                                        00-35283

TO

_____

FROM

_____

DATE

_____

To all the Children and Parents

in the World

Thousands of people have been privileged
to catch glimpses of the past from their own
families, relatives or friends, passing along
generations of timeless realities in which
time dissolves and we enter a different
dimension.
This is the culture.
Culture remains hidden inside us reminding
ourselves of who we are.
However, memories vanish sometimes.
The wonders of bringing out those memories
that have vanished are so valuable that they
will make us the richest people on earth
and will connect us with the loved ones that
existed before our time and we will find
centuries of endless wealth.
Look for that wealth.
It is always waiting to be discovered by you.

The Garden

of My Childhood

In the new land far away from home one
summer, I planted a garden.
This was a garden of love.
The soil was hard in extreme and
the land was vast
but my hands were young and fast.
This was the garden of my childhood.
The tiny little seeds I spread
all over one by one,
and one morning under my amazed mind
and my very eyes, the little seeds opened up
under the glorious sun.
In the garden of my childhood...

The loving sun came faithfully
every morning during that summer
far away in time and space now,
and, with his loving wings
and his powerful rays, he kissed my flowers
one by one
in the garden of my childhood...
This garden was a monument to my far
away land.

"Friendship that flows from the heart cannot
be frozen by adversity, as the water that
flows from the spring cannot congeal in winter."

James Fenimore Cooper

Next year, Spring came and
my heart palpitated harder and harder every
morning when I saw the many new flowers
opening up right under my amazed eyes.
This was my newly discovered joy.
I got up early each morning and I called
everyone to come see the miracle of life;
the Roses, Sweet Peas and the Morning Star.
They were busy, but they will see, they said.

"I am only one; but still I am one.
I cannot do everything, but still I can do something.
I will not refuse to do the something I can do."

Helen Keller

The following Spring, I started earlier than
usual. There were so many weeds to pull.
Winter had come so strong and cold
and had accumulated so much debris.
But they will come this year, quietly I
murmured to myself.
I have to get ready soon and fast!
I have to prepare my garden for them!
I have to share this delight with the ones I
love!
By April my garden so naturally looked
majestic.
The aroma of the Roses filled every little
space
and challenged the other flowers to do the
same. The Tulips, the Jasmines, the Sweet
Peas and the others gracefully took the
challenge and opened up together in a
graceful and exotic dance.
They were all celebrating the uniqueness of
the time and I called again,
I needed so much to share with them.
They were busy, but they will see, they said.

"Do not save your loving speeches for your friends
 until they are dead;
Do not write them on their tombstones,
Speak them rather now instead."

Anna Cummins

I continued working every day in my garden
that Summer. Perhaps if I work harder and
make the garden convey my message more
clearly, they will be able to hear my voice
calling with love, I thought.
Please came to see my garden, I shouted,
while with my magic hoses I watered the
flowers one by one.
Perhaps if the flowers have a stronger scent,
they will be able to smell from far away.
They will come this weekend
to see the garden of my childhood.
You see, I built it so they can see how I
spent those years when they were not with
me in that land far away now in time.
I wanted them to feel what I feel when
thinking of my childhood, for I am able to
miraculously transcend the moment and
transport myself to the years when I was
with my parents.
My appreciation for toiling the soil began
when I was with my father long ago.
I was recruited to work with him in the
garden, but soon I learned that with him
I was safe.

That strong sense of a specific place in space has given me peace and immense contentment through the years.

"We've got this gift of love, but love is like a precious plant. You can't just accept it and leave it in the cupboard or just think it's going to get on by itself.
You've got to keep watering it; really look after it
And nurture it."

John Lennon

The sun came faithfully every morning
to spread his beautiful rays and to enhance
my senses.
I felt the awakening of the earth each day
in my garden. It was the most idyllic place.
The earth opened up to let the spirits go
and do good deeds to every human being.
I felt decades of love calling me to join the
crowd.
A celebration of faith, I called the event each
morning.
I wanted to be able to share this experience
with the ones I love the most.
To share with my children the core of my
existence was my goal.
My response to these surroundings, to the
moods and sounds of nature, was full of a
deep sense of personal symbolism,
so I wanted them to see it. I wanted them to
experience it with me.

"Go often to the house of thy friend; for weeds soon choke up the unused path."

Edda (Scandinavian Mythology)

Next Spring came late and this gave me time
to prepare myself for the work of love I was
planning for them to see.
That year I wanted to add other flowers
to the garden of my childhood.
I know she liked Daisies so very much.
Perhaps this is the secret that I forgot.
If I plant a whole ocean of Daisies, I
thought, she will come.
I missed her so very much.
I remembered when she was little and fast
carrying the tiny little purse hanging from
her beautiful shoulder; she picked up wild
flowers one by one and orderly
placed them in the bottom of her purse,
and opening her arms in a loving embrace
running to me she said, "Look mommy
what I have in my purse. I'll give you
some. These are for you and me to share."
She had all the secrets of the world in her
little purse.
How can I forget?

"I've never sought success in order to get fame
and money; it's the talent and the passion that counts in success."
Ingrid Bergman

True love always hurts, I know, and I was
tired after all the work,
but I continued planting Daisies for her.
I wanted to show her that those white, pure
flowers were my tribute to the little girl
who had became a wonderful woman
in her own way.
I wanted to share with her that garden–
the garden of love, promises and friendship–
the garden of my own youth.
I made an effort to add some Hydrangeas.
Perhaps they will grow very tall and she will
be able to see them from the distance, and
through the flowers tell me how she was
doing, I thought.
Now I know that life is a long journey
but some paths we must travel alone,
for they are lessons to make us strong.

"Friendship is a word the very sight of
which makes the heart warm."

Augustine Birrell

By the end of the Summer, when the sun
was weak and I was extremely tired,
I called again.
They were busy; they will see, they said.
The Daisies died one by one waiting for her
to come, and the other flowers, exhausted
by the waiting, died too.
And they did not see that year the garden of
my youth.
Quickly, in my desperation, I dried the rest
of the flowers that were still alive in the
garden. I made crafts for them to see how
glorious their garden was in the Summer.
The flower arrangements rested without a
life or soul on my working table until
somebody came one day and offered to take
them.

"We can easily forgive a child who is afraid
of the dark; the real tragedy of life is when
men are afraid of the light."

Plato

Next Spring I started earlier than usual.
They will come this year, I know, I repeated
to myself.
In my search to give her the best, I planted
ivy, She loves ivy, I repeated to myself.
She also loves the beautiful aroma of herbs.
She often cooks with plenty of them, so
under my kitchen window, I planted a full
section of herbs.
Perhaps they will perform the miracle.
Suddenly one morning my hands started to
hurt, but they continued working in the
garden. I needed to add other herbs.
There was so much to do in the garden of
my youth.
The Sweet Basil spurred so quickly.
The aroma of the Oregano and the
Rosemary was unforgettable
They invaded my senses.
Happily I sang. I spent the mornings and
evenings watering the garden,
and I called again.
They were busy, but they will see, they said.

"We live at a time when man believes himself
fabulously capable of creation, but he does
not know what to create."

Jose Ortega y Gasset

All the birds came to see my garden every morning. The seed eating finches were always working hard to get the juicy seeds. The woodpeckers were busy making me a tiny little fence. The hummingbirds screaming for honey and the black-capped chickadees dancing with their bright capes performed for each body in the garden their eternal steps.

Many varieties of migrating birds found a house and a place to stay as long as they wanted, and they thanked me with their unique songs each morning.

The sparrows had babies, and others did too, and my garden gave them shelter.

The songs of the sparrows, the blue jays with their handsome crests, and even a falcon filled the air each day.

They sang like a panpipe until the gloaming came.

The aroma of the mint made their songs sweeter and sweeter as the Summer was coming to an end.

"The expectations of life depend upon diligence.
The mechanic that would perfect his work
must first sharpen his tools."

Confucius

The garden of my youth was now so much like that garden in that far away land of my childhood.

The project was completed, I thought. But then I smiled and reminded myself that I will be always adding more flowers to enhance my creation according to my emotions.

The trees were maturing to a full splendor, and the flowers were establishing themselves at home.

Every aroma, every smell reminded me of that far-away place.

"It is unwise to be too sure of one's own wisdom.
It is healthy to be reminded that the strongest might weaken and
the wisest might err.

Mahatma Ghandi

The next season Spring came late.
Winter took longer than usual.
I started weeding and cleaning every corner
of the garden.
Perhaps this year will be the year, I thought.
I did not have the same energy, and I
noticed that my hands really hurt with every
weed that I pulled, so I bought some new
product, a weed killer, someone said.
I did not like to use chemicals, because it
may affect them.
I wanted to keep my garden pure and
natural. But there was no other way to
eradicate those resistant weeds.
In a few days my garden looked in its way
to be the best ever.
I planted a few new flowers, a few new
trees. Again my friends, all the birds, came
singing a new song for me.
Their melodies sounded like heaven opening
up all the tunes of a life time.

"Self-expression must pass into communication
for its fulfillment."

Pearl S. Buck

My husband built a patio to show his true love and unconditional devotion to my garden. He paved the floor with beautiful Mexican tiles. He added a water fountain for all the birds to bathe and drink the clear water running through the necks of the kissing doves guarding the fountain.

The frogs and the cricket invited themselves too, and we welcomed them although they were the unexpected guests.

Every evening even our casual conversations were enhanced by the presence of the fountain in our garden.

The hummingbirds also had a place to stay, and like in a little coffee shop, my husband provided plenty of sweet juice for them to drink during their quick flights through their accustomed daily itinerary.

"The first foundation of friendship is not the power of conferring benefits, but the equality with which they are received, and may be returned.

Junius

Our many friends, the birds, started coming closer and closer to the house each morning and, to our delight, also gathered with us around the fountain in the evening.
One, the bravest one, built a nest for his family inside a planter
because he so much liked the fountain.
He made this place his new home.
He liked the sweet sound of the water cradling his babies.
I added ferns and ivy all around the fountain.
Each evening, listening to the sound of the water running so pure and secure, we had tea under the shaded patio.
The water splashed and my husband and I laughed with tremendous love for each other.
The fountain, with its soft breezes, seemed to create an endlessly simple and yet magnificent bond between us.
If only they were here, everything would be perfect, I thought, while I listened to my husband speaking. All of a sudden, his voice sounding soft and distant, I heard their playing voices as when they were little.

This experience used to happen every time
that I found myself longing to see them.
I called my children and they promised to be
home soon.
We waited the entire Spring and the entire
Summer, but they did not come.
They had plans, they said.

"It began in mystery, and it will end in mystery,
but what a savage and beautiful country
lies in between."

Diane Ackerman

Early in the Fall, I decided to add wild flowers to the garden of my youth.

I had heard that adding some things out of the ordinary helps to change the course of life some times.

I had plenty of space behind the rope fence for a second garden, a wild one.

I immediately started by removing all existing grass and weeds. Then I carefully raked the seeds into the soil and planted bright Poppies, crisp blues, deep reds and soft pinks.

I wanted to have lots of color to brighten the space. I also planted White Baby's Breath, Bachelors Buttons, Black-eyed Susan, Blue Flax, California Bluebell, Calliopsis, Cosmos, Godetia, Sweet Alyssum, Sweet William.

But most of all, Baby's Breath. She always loved them.

I saw Baby's Breath and Daisies in the vase every time I visited her.

I watered the wild flower garden twice a day for one month. I didn't want the hot sun to hurt the tiny roots just coming out of the seeds so they could see the flowers next Spring…

"I never notice what has been done. I only
see what remains to be done."

Madame Curie

After all that hard work in the garden that
Fall, I wanted to rest.
But before resting, I called again. Perhaps by
Christmas, if they come,
they could still see some of the other flowers
from the Summer, I thought.
They were busy, they had plans, they said…

"I find as I grow older that I love those most whom I love first."
Thomas Jefferson

"The method for the culture of friendship
finds its best and briefest summary in
the Golden Rule."

Hugh Black

Finally Spring was knocking at my door.
I saw the wild flowers opening up to the
sun, coquettish, kissing him one by one.
There were so many! The colors were
exuberant, with such power that I kneeled
down whispering, "They are more splendid
than gold."
Both gardens represented my childhood and
my youth mixing together,
my world of imagination and creation.
They were a magic blend of my entire life.
They represented a bond of sentiments that
was the thread of my whole existence.
If they could only see, I thought.
Again I called and left messages,
but no one answered, no one responded...

"Affection can withstand very severe storms of vigor, but not a
long polar frost of indifference."

Sir Walter Scott

"Happy is the house that shelters a friend."

Ralph Waldo Emerson

Summer went by very fast. I was busy. I traveled a lot. I made myself a busy schedule so I didn't have time to share with others. I indulged myself in endless activities close at hand and also far apart.
The roads that I traveled were familiar and yet far. I began the days at five in the morning and ended them late at night.
Each morning I passed between farms and green forests. I also crawled through downtowns. I didn't want to stop at any time. I ate lunches and dinners in my car.
Sometimes I heard a voice saying, "Make time to think, my daughter, make time to eat."
Perhaps it was my mother from the distance warning me. I don't know.
Then on a well-known hill far ahead, I would see my garden and would smell the aroma.
Then every thing was fine in my mind. However, I was still missing them in my heart. I remembered that there was a time when they were little and traveling was a great adventure. I remembered those wonderful trips to Disneyland.

"When love is out of your life, you're through in a way.
Because while it is there it's like a motor that's going, you have
such vitality to do things, big things,
Because love is goosing you all the time."

Fanny Brice

Next Spring I felt so tired and so sad.
I spent hours thinking that perhaps they did
not want to see the garden of my youth.
They did not want to know how it was
where I lived in that far away land.
It was hard to get out of bed in the morning,
but I needed to work in the garden,
although I didn't know if I could any more.
But I got strength every day by opening the
albums and looking at the pictures when
they were little.
I called to see if she had plans to come this
year, but there was no answer.
I tried to communicate using the e mail, but
there was no response.
The entire Summer went by. I tried to enjoy
my garden, but I couldn't because I missed
them so very much.
I missed her, we were so close before she
became a woman.
What happened? I asked myself.
But there were no answers.
I couldn't find one.

"There is nothing more tragic than to find an individual bogged down in the length of life, devoid of breadth."

Martin Luther King, Jr.

The following morning it was very hard to get out of bed.

I missed her, I thought, and as I opened once more the pages of their childhood albums and I saw her pictures holding her little purse on her shoulder, I reflected on my work and asked myself if I had planted enough flowers in the garden?

Perhaps the Daisies didn't have enough color on them? Perhaps the ivy was not green or attractive enough?

Perhaps the garden of my childhood and youth was not what she wanted to see.

For a few days after Mother's Day, I couldn't go out to see the garden.

I blamed myself. I blamed my garden.

The Daisies once again were smiling at me and suddenly asked for the reason of my sadness. I couldn't respond.

The beautiful birds were still giving me their songs, but it was hard to hear them...

"It is worse than folly...not to recognize the truth,
for in it lies the tinder for tomorrow."

Pearl S. Buck

My husband said one morning: "I bought some beautiful trees for you to plant: cherries, walnuts, avocados, and some plums. And I want to thank you for those beautiful roses you place on my nightstand every morning. I smell the aroma from far away coming home from work and this gives me strength."

"I don't want to plant any more," I said. "I just want to be in bed..."

As I lay down in bed that morning, I thought about loyalty and self forgetting devotion. And as Woodrow Wilson once said, "The object of love is to serve, not to win." Perhaps what I had wanted all that time, in building a garden for my children and in wanting to share with them my childhood and youth, was to make them a little more like me. However, this is not what they wanted. I knew I didn't need to win. I only wanted to share with them a piece of my life. I missed my beautiful daughter so much. If she can only come, it is fine that she does not see my garden, I thought, and I fell asleep for a long time.

"Courage is the price that life exacts
for granting peace."

Amelia Earhart

The following day a visitor came to my door.
I opened and he smiled with a smile of a
million years. He seemed somehow familiar
deep in my mind; looking into the center of
my eyes, he said, "Can I see your garden?"
"How do you know about my garden?" I
replied. He did not answer, but followed me
instead. In silence he looked at every flower
and nodded.
The birds noticed his presence. Singing, they
gathered around him, and he smiled as he
gently touched and praised them.
I asked again, "How do you know about my
garden?"
He seemed not to be listening at first.
I waited while he took a deep breath of air.
When he opened his lips to respond, he
paused again, and in a whisper, he
responded: "I knew about your garden even
before you built it. My friends the
birds for whom you built the bird houses
kept me informed of its progress all along. I
heard their call every morning after you fed
them." And he continued saying: "You see,
in your ever lasting search for your own
person, you wanted to build a garden to

show your children who you were before they knew you, before they became part of you so they could better understand the real you."

"True friends, like ivy and the wall. Both stand together, and together fall."

Thomas Carlyle

"The truth is a snare; you cannot have it without
being caught. You cannot have the truth
 in such a way that you catch it, but only in such a way that it
catches you."

Soren Kierkegaard

I looked deep into myself and I nodded without attempting to speak. Wisely again he spoke. "They are adults now, you see. True happiness is the enjoyment of one's self in the different stages of your own life." I started to see the reality after all these years of waiting. "Your children are building their own gardens now. They have their own flowers, their own memories. This is your garden and you must enjoy it." After pausing for air, he added: "Remember when your mother wanted to read to you about her garden in her far away land?" Suddenly everything came to my mind and as in a crystal vision, I found myself in a familiar place. I gazed up at the mountains, at the flowers around me, and did the only thing I know how to do in this situation. I smiled. Is this the force that is bidding me to do the same I wondered to myself. Then I remembered. When I decided to build a garden, it was the garden of my childhood. I wanted to feel close to that far away home, to smell the aromas of that time, to feel that age again. Or perhaps to avenge an old grievance with my mother during my youth.

As I added more trees, flowers and herbs, I felt so amazed with my creation, that I wanted to share it with my children. I wanted them to see what I saw.

"He who wishes to teach us a truth should not tell it to us, but simply suggest it with a brief gesture, a gesture which starts an ideal trajectory in the air along which we glide until we find ourselves at the feet of the new."

Jose Ortega y Gasset

As I suddenly saw the picture of all these years of waiting for them to see my garden, I reacted and thought, I have not enjoyed my own garden alone. At this moment a second world that I had never seen before made itself known to me.

This world was full of contentment and joy. It showed me who really I am. It showed me vivid moments of my whole life. I understood that I am here for a reason and the gardens that I created during my life time always will be shared by my loved ones. I promised to myself to accept the nature of my existence. I promised to myself that as long as I lived, I will tend to my own garden.

"It's life, isn't it? You plow ahead and make it.
And you plow on and someone passes you.
Then someone passes him. Time levels."

Katherine Hepburn

Today and each day I need to remember to treasure peace and tranquility. The memories of my own life that I have treasured so much won't go away. I was so afraid that some day they would disappear so I wanted so much to reproduce and share them with the ones I love, with my children so they can help me to remember in my old age. But now I know. My memories are with me forever. God will help me to remember them. I started to enjoy my garden again. I just have to close my eyes and smell the Sweet Peas, the Roses, the Jasmines, and see the Gladiolus of the gardens of my childhood and youth.

"The past is a ghost; the future a dream;
and all we ever have is now."

Bill Cosby

There is no end...